Lee Lister is a Bid and Program Manager with more than 25 years consultancy experience and 16 years bid management experience ranging from small bids to large international and country infrastructure bids. On the internet she is known as "**The Bid Manager**".

Whilst working in the Far East she became a recognized expert on preparing and evaluating large World Bank Bids (infrastructure and business process projects within developing countries). She also consulted on setting the World Bank Bid Evaluation Criteria. This expertise was acknowledged by an invitation to be the principle speaker at an International Business Development Conference in Washington, USA.

She has also consulted at very senior level and with government officials in numerous countries Her experience encompasses, bid management, bid evaluation, bid training, consultancy and program management. She is a prolific published author and can easily be found on major search engines.

First published in Great Britain in 2008. Previous incarnations were sold as ebooks from 2002.

ISBN: 978-1-907551-02-4

Other books available include:
Proposal Writing For Smaller Businesses
Profitable New Quilting Business
Profitable New Face Painting Business
Profitable New Bottled Water Business
Profitable New T Shirt Printing Business
Profitable New Cake Decoration Business
Profitable New Manicurist Business

Profitable New Party Selling Business

Learn how to set up a profitable business, understand how to overcome the strains and stresses of a new company and become a Successful Entrepreneur

www.StartMyNewBusiness.com

This book is dedicated to my daughter Kerry Lister for whom I have always strived to be my best.

Contents

Legal Notice

We do not believe in get rich quick schemes. We do believe that business is equal parts of inspiration, hard work and luck. We ensure that every book that we sell will be interesting and useful to our clients. Every effort has been made to accurately represent our service and it's potential. Any testimonials and examples used are not intended to represent the average purchaser and are not intended to guarantee that anyone will achieve the same or similar results

Please remember that each individual's success depends on his or her background, dedication, desire, and motivation. As with any business endeavour, there is an inherent risk of loss of capital. **There is no guarantee that you will earn any money**.

This book will provide you with a number of suggestions you can use to better guarantee your chances for success. **We do not and cannot guarantee any level of profits.**

Profitable New Party Selling Business

This book is written with the warning that any and every business venture contains risks, and any number of alternatives. We do not suggest that any one way is the right way or that our suggestions are the only way. On the contrary, we advise that before investing any money in a business venture you seek counselling and help from a qualified accountant and/or attorney.

You read and use this book on the strict understanding that you alone are responsible for the success or failure of your business decisions relating to any information presented by our company

Biz Guru Ltd.

Introduction

Believe it or not a Party Selling Business is one of the easier types of businesses to start up – proving you have the right product of course! Party Selling – sometimes called party planning became internationally renowned when companies such as Tupperware and Avon became very profitable very quickly.

Party Selling involves, as the name implies, holding parties of friends and acquaintances with the intention of not only having fun, but also selling products that you enjoy to them! It is one of the most enjoyable and least stressful ways of selling that there is. Of course, as mentioned above, you still have to have some good products to sell; otherwise you quickly become very unpopular with your friends.

A recent questionnaire, circulated among hundreds of successful direct sales merchandisers across the country asked this questions: "If you were to start over today, knowing what you know now and could choose the one method of merchandising that would make you really rich in the shortest period of time, which would you select?" Of these questionnaires returned, 94% stated they would go The Party Selling Method. Reasons often cited include "ease of start up", "low cost", "high propagation" etc.

Party Selling should not be confused with network marketing – which is illegal in many countries. You are not selling to other people the chance to hold their own parties – but selling a great bona fida product. It is true that some Party Selling companies also encourage people to hold their own parties, but this is to "spread the word", not to network market.

The clever Party Selling operators hold motivational sales meetings for their distributors about once a month. During these meetings, they are teaching them how to recruit new hosts or host teams in order to quickly spread the word about the new products.

How It Works

You employ one or more distributors, whose role is to find hosts, get a Selling Pack to them, support them during or before a party, collect orders and the corresponding money, and finally provide the host with the products sold so that they can pass it on to the party attendees.

A host can be any person who is agreeable to holding a sales party at their house. Almost always, this person is rewarded for having the party with a percentage of the total business or an agreed upon special merchandise gift.

The host invite friends, neighbours and relatives to the party and demonstrates the products to them.

Often in a party atmosphere so that people do not feel that they are being pressured. They then take orders and the required money and pass it on to the distributor. Once they receive their guest's products they give them to them.

Here's the kind of money you can realize with this business: Say you have ten distributors, and each one arranges only five parties a month, and each party does $200 in gross business. That's a total of $10,000 per month in total volume. And from that total volume, you make only 30%. Figure it out for yourself. This would give you a personal income of $3,000 for thirty days in which you did no more than hold one or two motivational sales meetings and supplied a lot of product!

With a good product and a lively party you are almost guaranteed to gain at least one or two more hosts for future parties and those future parties will provide still more hosts. So you can see how quickly the word is spread!

Possible Problems

There are several main problems that you will face:

- Your product is not good enough to encourage party buying.
- You do not have a strong enough or wide enough product range suitable for a party environment.
- Your product is not suitable for a party environment – being too big, too expensive or too difficult to store and distribute.
- You have such a large range of products on offer that stocking and distributing becomes a major problems as does setting up host's sample ranges.

As you can see the choice of product that you wish to sell is very important so we will discuss this in length late in the book.

Right now we need to ensure that your business is set up correctly and that you have a strong business base from which to start. This is most important in any business, but with the speed that Party Selling takes off, and the problems of distribution and collecting funds, it is even more important.

Will I Succeed?

You've got a great idea, you are pretty sure that what you have will sell; you've even got some cash together. Have you got what it will take to succeed? What else do you need?

Vision: You must be able to see where you are going and what the future will hold. See what others are not able to see and build your business on these visions.

Courage: The ability to act upon your vision despite having doubts. The readiness to give up job security and a planned future; for the chance of making a success with your new business. This takes courage.

Strategy: Having the courage to act upon your vision, you now need to build your strategies. You will need a business and a marketing strategy. These are the formulas that you will use to drive forward and manage your business.

Planning Skills: To ensure that you reach your vision, you need copious amounts of planning. Planning how you will reach your targets, how you will meet new changes and challenges and how you will improve your business. You will need a business plan and a marketing plan.

Researching: Having decided what your business is going to be, then you will need to find out who will want to buy from your business and at what price. This takes a fair amount of researching.

Conceptualizing: Knowing what you want to sell and to whom, you now need to define your products and services. Brainstorm different things that you associate with your company. Include everything, good and bad, until you are out of ideas. Keep in mind that ideas generate ideas. Write everything down, this is how you move your company forward. Use this period to design your products, what you want your company to look like and how you want it to be perceived by your customers.

Creativity: You will need the ability to think outside of the box. Keep ahead of your competitors by coming up with new, unusual and unique concepts and solutions to their needs. You will need to create marketing materials, packaging and sales pitches – all will need verbal and visual creativity.

Determination: Along the way you will come across many hurdles and set backs, you will need to dig deep, make your changes and keep going. Determination and the belief in your visions and plans will keep you on the road to success.

Humour: When all the world seems against you and all seems to be going wrong, when your customers seem to be your worst enemy then you need a sense of humour to carry you forward.

Lastly you need good luck!

A Successful Business Start up

Right you have sorted out your business ideas, you are ready to go ahead and you know what you want to sell and to whom. Now you need your business structure. These are all the things that make up your business. They include:

 • **Legal Base:** This includes such factors as your licenses, insurances and setting up your company.

 • **Your Market:** You need to decide who you want to market your services to and where they will be.

 • **Your Services:** You now need to decide what services you are going to offer to these people, how you would like to package them and what prices you wish to charge.

 • **Your Premises:** Look around for your new premises, preferably in the middle of your potential market. Remember that central to your success is the position you choose for your business. Foot traffic past your door and many potential customers within a short journey from your new business is vital to you finding customers.

 • **Web Site:** Most businesses have them now – so even if you don't want to set one up now – at least buy and hold onto your domain name – in case someone else gets hold of it.

 • **Your Business Plan:** Whether you are looking for funding or not – a business plan is the foundation of a new business.

• **Your Funding:** You should now take your business plan and look around for funding, starting with your Bank.

• **Your Staff:** Good staff that reflect your business ideals are vital so spend some time spend some time finding the best staff you can.

• **Marketing:** So important and so difficult to get right. Start with a good marketing strategy and go from there.

• **Grand Opening:** Make sure you make a splash and attract as much curiosity as possible.

Your Business Framework

When starting a business of what ever kind, large or small, there is a always a require framework or scaffolding that you have to set up. Not only does this make your business much more effective, but it also saves you from a lot of embarrassing and costly problems. When you start up your business, remember to tick off the 10 items below and you will have a very sound start to your business. Here is your framework:

- **Business Name.** Choose an appropriate name that sums up what your business stands for. It has to be unique – try and ensure that a suitable domain name is also available as you will probably want a web site as well. The owner of an established web site might cause problems if you give your brick based business the same name – so be careful in your choice.

- **Your Business Entity.** Obtain professional advice as whether to the best way to set up your business as a limited company, partnership etc. Then register your company.

- **Patents and Trademarks**. If you have unique products then you need to ensure that you have registered your patents before your start trading. Similarly any product names, mottos, selling tags etc should be trademarked. Take professional advice on how to do this.

- **Licenses and Permits.** Ensure that you have all the licenses and permits that you are legally required to have.

• **Insurance.** You may think that you don't need this but you do and will. So take out property, business, vehicle liability, staff and disaster insurance. A good broker can advise you.

• **Taxes.** A necessary evil I am afraid. Register with your local tax collector. Set up a good accounting system and hire a good accountant.

• **Employment Laws.** Establish what you local employment laws are and ensure that you adhere to them. Set up employee guidelines and handbooks. Make sure you hire and fire legally.

• **Banking.** Visit your local banks and find the best business bank account and credit card for you business. Always keep your business and personal spending separate.

• **Business Plan.** This is your carefully written plan on how you want your company to operate, what you want to sell, where and to whom. It includes your business and marketing strategy as well as your financial standing and projections. This is the foundation of your business.

• **Liquid Cash.** Ensure that you have enough money to carry your through the first few months of your business as well as any foreseeable troublesome times ahead.

How Much Does It Cost To Start A Business?

You've got your business idea, think that you will be able to get a good loan and even have your business plan being written but…. The one big burning issue is – How much does it cost to start a business?

Well you first of all have to be realistic and understand that you are unlikely to make a profit within the first six months of business – so you should also budget for your first six months running costs. So here is your shopping list:

1) Purchase of lease/franchise/premises. This will include any Realtor fees, deposits and other legal expenses. Even party sellers need some kind of premises. To start with you can use a home office, but you are going to need somewhere to hold all that stock and marketing materials that you will soon need.

2) Cost of fit out and purchase of new equipment. This will include any work that needs to be done on your premises as well as any equipment you have to buy in order to start and run your business. Often you can lease equipment in order to mitigate high start up costs. This also includes a car or van to deliver your stock to your distributors.

3) Six months worth of advertising and marketing. This will be particularly high at the start as you establish your business.

Factor in some cold calling as well as a launch party or opening day. Marketing will include a lot of local advertising in order to attract good distributors.

4) Legal, licensing and banking costs. Your business will need to be set up correctly, licensed and have a good bank account. Sadly all of these require money. You may also need a payment processing service to use credit cards.

5) Staff costs for six months. Staff will be the basis of providing good service to your new customers. Make sure that you have enough money put aside to find them, train them and keep them! Much of your staff costs will be on a commission basis but you will still require admin staff and one or two "on staff" distributors and maybe warehouse staff as well. They will all want to be paid, often before you get paid for your sales.

6) Uniforms, office and marketing supplies, packaging etc. You will need to establish your brand. This means that your staff will need uniforms or at the least business cards and name tags. You will need brochures, adverts etc. If appropriate you will also need standardized packaging and documentation. Your office will also need office equipment and supplies. You should also budget for designing your logo, brochures and adverts if you cannot do this yourself.

7) Stock and supplies – to keep you going for six months. This is a big expense because if you have 10 hosts they all need a core stock from which to sell from.

8) Maintenance for six months – your equipment will also need to keep going for six months. This includes your cars, computers, printers, copiers etc. Budget for a lot of printing ink!

9) Any loans that you have will also have to be paid. Again look at least at six months or until you break even and can pay the loan.

10) Your salary for six months – lastly you will need to pay your own bills and maintain your family during this time. You should expect that for a short while your standard of living will go down.

Add this up and add 10% for contingency and some good luck.

Check List For Starting A New Business

Y ou are ready to give up your job to start your new business, or even scarier, sink your savings into your new business. You just want to make sure that you have done everything possible to succeed, here is a check list for you.

1. Legal Stuff:

- Do you have a memorable business name and the associated domain name?
- Do you have a legal name and business entity?
- Have you got all your licences?
- Have you got all you certificates such as health and fire?
- Have you registered everything you need to?
- Have you told the tax department and got your numbers and details?
- Are all your shares, statutory meetings etc correct?
- Do you have all the patents and trademarks you need?
- Do you have the legal documents on your premises – leases, sales, mortgages etc.?
- Do you have all the posters and legal manuals etc that you need?

2. Strategies and Planning:

- Do you have your Business Plan written?
- Do you have a Business Strategy?
- Do you have a Marketing Strategy?
- Have you decided upon what Business Model you will use?

3. Protection:

- Do you have your insurances for you, the company, liabilities, staff, premises and vehicles?
- Have you got health insurance for you and staff if necessary?
- Do you have your pension set up?

4. Finances:

- Are your finances in place and have you signed all the forms necessary?
- Do you have enough and on the right terms?
- Have you got your bank set up?
- Do you have your credit/debit card and payment processor set up?

5. Premises:

- Are your premises/office ready and equipped?
- Are all the utilities that you need connected – gas, electric, phone, broadband etc.?
- Do you have all the vehicles, computers and machinery that you need?

6. Staff:

- Do you have all the staff you need?
- Are they trained or ready to be trained?
- Do you have the necessary uniforms?

7. Marketing and Services:

- Have you checked who your potential market is and where these customers are hiding?
- Have you ensured that what you are selling is really, really what your proposed customers want?
- Do you have your pricing and upgrading sorted out?
- Do you have your branding sorted out?
- Do you have your starting marketing materials?
- Do you have standard replies to customer enquiries, invoices, receipts, business cards and letter heads sorted out?

The Nasties

Tax, Insurance, Licences and Certificates these are the nasties of your business and all of them are compulsory! Look up your local state/county/country web site to see what licences and certificates you will need. Similarly your country's tax web site will tell you what taxes you will need to pay, how you register to pay them and what forms you will need to fill in to become legal. Don't attempt to work without them – there goes the way to a world of misery. Tax officials in particular, are trained to find and collect unpaid taxes and these are always combined with extra costs and penalties.

Operating your business in some countries will require you and your staff to be licensed before you can start work. This should be displayed on your premises or available for view by your customers.

Common Business Mistakes.

All entrepreneurs have to learn from their own mistakes as they build their business, but wouldn't it be great to have some one tell you what the common mistakes are and how to avoid them? You Want a Successful Business – So Don't Do This!

- **Believing that you will start earning straight away**. All businesses take time to establish themselves – even internet based ones. People need to know where you are, what you sell and most importantly, that they can trust your company to deliver what it promises. Expect to spend at least 6 months working away at your business before you break even – sometimes longer.

- **Believing that you can set up a business and it continually earns for you.** Even a very profitable business needs continual management to ensure that your profit does not erode. Your products and marketing need to continually change to meet the changing circumstances in the real world.

- **Believing that you can earn whilst you are aware from the office.** Even if you fully automate your business and hire really good staff, there is always an element of "while the cat is away". That is why there are so many "absent owner" sales.

• **Being a single product company.** As good as your product may be, markets and tastes will change and so must you. If your product is very good – other companies will quickly take action to seize your market share by bringing in similar products at cheaper prices.

• **Not offering upgrades and enhancements.** It is far easier and cheaper to sell to existing customers. You do this by offering upgrades and enhancements to their existing products. You should have a group of products at several increasing price points.

• **Relaxing after you success.** Businesses need continual effort, management and improvements. Although a product launch is hard work, you should start on your next product shortly afterwards. This will give you sustainable success and several income streams.

• **Believing that a business can be established with little capital.** Marketing, infrastructure purchases, stock, advertising and staff all cost money and must be purchased in order to make a profit. Cash flow kills more business than anything else.

• **Not investing in your staff.** Your staff are the public face of your business. They should be well trained, knowledgeable and well dressed as well as fully motivated to sell on your behalf.

• **Believing that you know all you have to**. Your competitors may have been in the business longer than you have, your customers may be very knowledgeable. Meeting customer needs is a constantly changing landscape and you need to keep up to date on the latest trends and technology. You need to be able to project yourself as an expert in the field you work in. If you do not have this knowledge then learn it or buy it in!

• **Believing in Get Rich Quick Schemes:** A good business is established by part inspiration, part perspiration and just a little bit of luck!

Whilst the above are pertinent to every business there are a few that are special to the Party Selling business. These are:

• **Branding.** It is important that your goods are recognised and that they have a good image. This helps spread the word about your products! Otherwise why would the hosts wish to hold a party? Spend on your brand, its worth it!

• **Not motivating** your distributors or hosts sufficiently. Selling on commission only is very hard work, it must be rewarding and the hosts should feel that they will benefit from it. Your distributors, particularly at the beginning will be chasing around looking for hosts, doing a lot of mileage, delivering stock in the evenings and looking after hosts. So they need motivating and reward well. Good distributors and hosts will grow your business exponentially so you must look after them.

• **Distribution problems.** Once you get started you will have several parties being held each week, and the geographic area will quickly spread. You *must* ensure that you can not only get the purchased products to the hosts, quickly and efficiently but that they also need selling kits, upgrades, renewals and new products delivered to them.

• **Stock Holdings.** With distribution problems comes stock holding problems, the more products you have, the more stock you must have. For example, think of 20 product lines spread over 50 hosts means that you need 20x50 = 1,000 items just in the Selling Packs. Then you need actual stock to deliver to your customers. If you have different sizes and colours this figure goes up even more!

You also have to think of your hosts' Selling Packs as "dead goods" as they cannot be sold as they are handled so much. Many party sellers ask the hosts for deposits for the Selling Packs or ask them to buy them at a nominal rate. It is very important that you work out how much stock you need – no more and no less!

• **Selling Processes.** With many hosts and distributors all handling stock and money. You need some efficient and robust processes in hand to manage both stock and money so that they don't get muddled and lost. You also need to consider how to handle refunds. Many companies lose money and even go out of business because they don't get their stock paid for or don't get the paid product to the party goer!

Learn these lessons well, avoid the mistakes at all costs you should save valuable time and resources by doing things right the first time. I think that you are ready for your first party now!

Choosing Your Products

Party selling will not work for every product that you have. You products must be suitable and for this they must have the following attributes:

- Be small enough so that numerous items can be displayed within someone's house.
- Be of a general interest to the party goers.
- Be of a price that they can be bought as a "no prior thought" purchase.
- Their wholesale price should be low enough to enable large stocks to be held.
- Be readily available from manufacturers but have some scarcity value and thus not found generally in local shops or chain stores.
- Be able to be handled by numerous people without breaking or getting excessively dirty.
- Have several price points and preferably upgrades.
- Have a good perceived value and be of sufficient quality to encourage multiple and repeat purchases.

Ideal items are therefore:

- Of an individual brand that is not sold elsewhere.
- Make-up, household goods, jewellery, toys, clothes, pet goods, food, cleaning products, ornaments, crafts etc.

Party Selling should not be confused with seminars and promoting services and products to small, discrete audiences.

If you can find a product that has not been sold by party planning before then you have a great start to your business. This is how Anne Summers started after all.

Try and be a little "out of the box" with your thoughts. Yet more candles, jewellery, clothes, cleaning products etc. can be a little boring unless you have some really different. You will be really challenged if you go up against Avon or Tupperware for instance but your scented pillows and shawls may be more interesting.

Think: Would you go to a party that is demonstrating your product?

Pricing Your Product

Pricing is so important to the success of your business. Too high and people will just go to the party, have a good time and a good look, but will leave without buying. Too low and you may not make a profit, your host will receive little to repay them for their effort and your party goers may think they are of a low quality.

When pricing your product look at the following:

- Your price should be such that a party goer can afford the "luxury" of purchasing it and trust enough to leave that money with the host to pay for it.
- The price should be at the correct level so that collecting the party proceeds and banking it is not onerous.
- The money collected from a party should not be tempting enough to encourage shrinkage or loss of a host. So don't get them to collect enough that you may not hear from them again!

Your profit is decided by:

- The sales price minus your host costs minus your distributor costs is your sales price.
- Your costs will be the distribution costs plus office and travel costs. From this you should make enough profit to pay yourself a decent salary and be able to expand your business.

Profitable New Party Selling Business

Your distribution and storage costs will be high and you will be paying two sets of commission (host and distributor), but you will not have shop costs.

You should set some money aside to build up your brand image by advertising and training your distributors. People are more likely to come to a party if they know the product and what it does or can do.

By managing your stock levels to an optimum level, you should be able to keep the costs to a minimum.

Choosing Your Distributors

Your distributors are the people who will be managing the growth of your company as well as managing the hosts and recruiting more hosts. Your distributor can also be a host or they can be independent.

Some Party Selling business models employ only hosts as distributors and they pay them only commission. Whilst your costs will be lower, your expansion will be much slower. This is because the hosts will tend to working for "pocket money" or part time work.

A full time distributor paid a small salary plus commission will work much harder to find hosts – as they find more hosts they earn more.

You can find local hosts by advertising in Job Centres, in local papers and on local advertising boards. You can also incentivise your hosts by promoting some of them as well.

You should look for gregarious, well organises sales orientated people who don't mind working in the evenings. It stands to reason that they should understand your products as well as how to motivate people and be great at networking!

Branding, Packaging And Other Stuff

B randing is so important. It is how people recognise your company and what you are selling. People will more readily hold parties for companies that they recognise and buy products that understand and know.

Your brand is so much more than your logo; it is your company name, your web site and the colours that you use. Everything that your customers and staff see should be "stamped" with your company brand and be instantly recognised as belonging to your company. So let us look at where your will be using your brand.

Party Items

Your potential customers should see your company image, logo and contact details on the following items:

- **Name tags:** to be used by the party goers, hosts and distributors.
- **Display boards:** to display your items. You should also include hangers etc as needed.
- **Catalogues:** Every party goer should have a catalogue so that they can see your entire product range. This should have your contact details, how to order, a reference number so that the host can be credited with commission and your web site.

The Selling Pack

Your host's Selling Pack should include the following, all branded:

- Products – enough to show your range and different price points. They should be in good order and replaced as required.
- Product information – so that your host can sell them effectively.
- Catalogues – to give to the party goers.
- Party Invites – to invite the guests.
- Order Forms – to collect the orders.
- Commission list – so that the host knows what they can earn.
- Host requests – to give to the party goers if they wish to be a host.
- Party booking form – for party goers and host to book another party.

Packaging

It stands to reason that all your packaging, including that used in delivering your items, should be stamped with your company name, logo, phone number and web site.

All packaging should include further Order Forms, stamped with the relevant host, and a catalogue.

Invoices and Order Forms

They should have your company details, contact details and web site as well as your logo.

Marketing Material

Once again you should market such that your company and how to contact it, is instantly recognisable. How and where you advertise should also back up your brand image. If you are selling family friendly items then you would not advertise in a "lad's mag" for example.

The Party

Now we have your business set up, your processes sorted out and you have decided what you want to sell. Let's look at a party. Every party should be planned, and follow a prescribed format or agenda. This is because without a plan, it will just be a gathering of people wasting time at your home instead of theirs. You must have a plan to know what to do next in order to achieve the desired results. Having a "pattern" is also the easiest way to teach others to duplicate your success, and the idea of following a successful formula is a proven method of making the most sales in the least time.

1. **Phase one** is the greeting and get-acquainted time slot - about thirty minutes. The hostess greets the guests as they arrive, prints a name tag for each, introduces them around, gives them a catalogue, points out the refreshments, and leads them into conversation with the other guests.

2. **The second phase** is the "game-playing" portion of your part. This phase is used to relax everybody and get them involved in the party. It should last about 15 to 20 minutes.

3. **Next comes** the merchandise presentation by the host, who shows and describes each item on display. Ask different guests to try on or inspect particular items and show the others what these articles look like in use.

The length of time spent on this phase of the party will depend in large part on how much merchandise you have on display, but generally, you shouldn't spend more than about 20 minutes showing and describing your merchandise. Then give your guests about 10 to 15 minutes to personally inspect and try on/inspect the items that have aroused their interest.

Party Administration

Be sure you have name tags for your guests, and a couple of felt tip marking pens. And don't forget the Order Forms. These should be standard two-piece self-carbon Order Forms - one copy for your customer and the other for your files. The best idea is to have printed your own Order Forms with your logo, contact details and sales message printed on them.

Another item to remember is your merchandise catalogues. Be sure you have a good supply on hand, all printed with your logo and address.

You could purchase these items and stamp your own details on them – but this does not instil anywhere near as much confidence in your company.

Setting Up Your Party

To get your start in this fabulous method of merchandising, become a host yourself. Give a few parties yourself, and learn the ropes.

Choose an evening for your party - any evening excepting Friday through the weekend. Generally 7:30 is the most convenient time for the greatest number of people. If it's inconvenient for whatever reason to hold a party in your home, arrange with a friend to hold the first couple of parties.

Make up a list of 30 to 60 people you can invite to the party. They can be friends, neighbours, relatives or people you know from work, even acquaintances with whom you do business such as the check-out clerk where you buy your groceries or people you meet at the bus stop on your way to work.

After formally inviting these people, you then call to remind them of the party at least a couple of days before the date of the party. This is important, because of the original 40 people you invite, at least 15 will not show because it slipped their minds, last minute circumstances that force a change in plans, and those that really weren't interested in the first place.

On the day of the party, get your merchandise display set up early. The party should be held in the largest room in the home - usually the living room - with the merchandise display the centre of attraction.

The merchandise should be set out on a sturdy table covered with a good white or light coloured cloth, and the merchandise should be arranged by group or type - the jewellery items together; perfumes, bath oils and colognes together; crystal together, and so on.

Try to put some imagination and showmanship into your merchandise display. This will have the effect of making your merchandise look much more valuable than it actually is. Those that do put flair into their merchandise displays find that it increases their sales by as much as 25 percent over an ordinary showing.

For instance, a high intensity light focused on the display will cause jewellery to sparkle, the stainless steel to gleam, and the brass-ware to glimmer like valuable heirlooms.

Another idea would be to tack a piece of velvet onto a 4 by 6 foot piece of ply wood and use it to display rings, earrings, necklaces, watches or any other similar items.

In jewellery and clothes sales, another idea is to hang a mirror on a wall near the merchandise display. If you or your host has room, you might want to set up a card table, covered with an expensive looking piece of material, place a dressing table type mirror on this table, with a chair available for your guests to sit at the table while they try on the various items. The guests then make their selections after determining how each item looks on them.

Regardless of what you do to make it easier for your guests to select and buy, a hand mirror is an absolute must whenever you're showing jewellery. It would be wise to have several hand mirrors available - two for your merchandise display table, and an extra one on the "admiration" table.

Besides your merchandise display, be sure also you're organized with your refreshments. These usually consist of coffee, tea, soft drinks, biscuits or other "nibble" items. The host usually makes arrangements in advance for one of the guests to assist with the serving of refreshments.

About a half hour before your guests are due to begin arriving, turn on all the lights in the room where the party is to be held. This will give the room a bright, warm feeling conducive to a party kind of atmosphere.

Eliminate any and all noises from other rooms in your home that might distract the attention of your guests. Be sure to turn off all the radios, stereo and TV sets.

You should mingle and converse with the guests during this time period in order to answer specific questions or explain the possible uses of an item, where it might look good in the buyer's home, and any interesting titbits relating to where an item came from, how it was made, or the satisfaction of an earlier buyer.

When you seem to have answered all the questions and everyone appears to have made their selections, start writing orders. Don't hesitate to ask for orders. Writing orders should take about 15 minutes, and then you should let the party begin to winding down.

When you give a gift to the host for having the party, the presentation should be a special ceremony staged with all the "Show Biz" flair you can muster, at the end of your merchandise showing. However, when your gift is a cash award, carry your presentation over to the next party and make a big production of it as well. Don't forget to invite the "guest of honour" to your next scheduled party for the big presentation.

During these presentations many of the other guests will be favourably impressed, and as a consequence will ask you for details of becoming a host themselves.

During this time, mingle with your guests and anyone showing a spark of interest should be approached with an offer to serve as a future host. As each guest starts to leave, thank them for coming and walk with them to the door.

The total length of your party shouldn't be much more than two hours. Time and time again, it's been proven that you can do everything necessary, and make the most sales in this period of time. You lose effectiveness and make fewer sales with appreciably more or less time.

Recruiting New Hosts

There are a couple of proven ways to recruit new hosts or hosts from the people attending your party. First of all, watch the guests as they look over the merchandise, examine, admire and wish for something they don't quite have enough extra money to buy. When you've determined that a particular guest wants a specific item but can't quite fit it into the budget, simply take her aside to a secluded corner of the room, and explain privately that you're willing to give her the item she has been looking at and wanting, if she will agree to invite her friends and relatives to a party in her home.

This approach works almost every time, and your only expense is the wholesale price of the item you give her as the free gift.

The second sure-fire approach is to offer a cash incentive. You do this by offering to allow 5% to 10% of the total sales volume resulting from the party staged for you by this type of new recruit. There's a plus factor for you on this one, because you'll be getting the enthusiastic participation of the host on the selling side. Once you've explained to them how your program works, they'll generally do everything they can to make the party a huge success, and thereby increase their pay for the evening.

Actually, your recruiting efforts should begin when you start taking orders. Every person you talk with should be offered the opportunity to hold a party of his or her own. Then just before the party begins breaking up, ask your guests as a group if any of them would be interested in holding a similar party in his or her home. You ask those who voice an interest to stay over for a few minutes in order to work out the details.

You should have an Appointment Book for this scheduling. Simply ask what date would be favourable for them, mark that date in the book, along with the name, address and telephone number. Then assure each that you'll call in the next day or two to work out the details.

Most people tend to feel Party Selling merchandising is exclusive to women, but don't you believe it! It's true that women generally establish themselves more rapidly than men with this kind of sales operation, but over the long haul, there are just as many men operating successful Party Selling sales operations as there are women.

A husband and wife partnership is an ideal working arrangement. An acquaintance, girlfriend or relative will often work out just as successfully. The basic requirement is simply that the "couple" must function as a team, with the individual talents of one complementing those of the other.

Advertising

Many Party Selling merchandisers use a letter. They write a letter extolling the fun and excitement of the parties, explaining briefly the opportunities to receive free gifts of their choice or big commission checks. Then they invite the letter recipients to call for complete details on how they can stage a party. These letters are usually printed in volume, and then slipped inside the covers of the catalogue the hosts give to each person attending the parties. Sometimes these letters are handed to each guest as the party breaks up.

Some party sellers also run small classified ads in the area newspapers. Their advertising plays up the opportunities available to make regular commission checks (extra income) simply by holding parties in their homes. People interested are invited to phone for more details. Response to this kind of ad is generally very good, with the conversion rate better than sixty percent!

As you get larger, you can afford more expensive advertising such as radio adverts or local magazine adverts to support your distributors or a major host.

Whilst Party Selling provides a generic growth it is important that you also advertise to capture those that have not heard of you!

Administration

Administration is very important. Without good distraction your company will quickly disintegrate into chaos and you won't know who has what and who needs to pay for items and who needs them to be delivered. Your administration should include ways of controlling or managing the following:

- Managing your host's Selling Pack – giving out, auditing, collecting, updating, refreshing.
- Collecting orders and money from the host.
- Collecting purchased items from stock.
- Delivering purchased items to host.
- Banking money.
- Managing returns.
- Managing enquiries and complaints.
- Invoice and bill payment.
- Accounts and book keeping including, payroll, banking, taxes and VAT.
- Purchasing and auditing stock. At least once a year and preferably quarterly, stock must be checked against your accounts.
- Salary and commission payments.
- Staff training and development.
Product improvements and upgrades.

It may seem a lot, but if you start small and get yourself a good accounts package, a good accountant and bank manager it is a lot easier.

Putting Your Business On The Internet

Just about anyone can put a web site up on the internet and now days it is quite easy. You have two choices as how to set up your website:

- As a shop window for your company, with contact details etc.
- As a fully working site with ecommerce facilities.

Which ever option you choose, you first need a god domain name. Go to a good domain provider like enom, godaddy, namecheap NOT registerfly and spend under $10 on a domain. Choose a domain name that has the word dating, love etc in it. This will help with your search engine positioning as well as act as a memory jog to your potential customers.

As A Shop Window

Hop over to hostgator or similar and then buy a monthly hosting account. With that will come a site maker - where you can easily set up a web site using one of thousands of templates. You can add payment processor linkages, forums etc.

The only problem you will have is you want to sell promote or talk about illegal activities, terrorist activities or sex! Also if you want a high usage activity such as Myspace etc.

As A Full Site

You will probably need to get this especially written and designed for you. Put your project on sites like guru/elance/scriptlance etc and find a competitive quote.

Get yourself a PayPal account or similar so that you can take payment on your web site. This is much more secure and quicker than taking checks.

Factors To Remember

Always consider your target market when designing your web site. Include some helpful information about your subject matter but nothing that will give away what you are trying to sell!

Ensure that your contact details can be freely found and that details of your company and services are clearly set out.

As you will be asking for money before you deliver something – make your potential customer feel comfortable making payment and tell them what will happen next.

Respond to all enquiries and purchases very quickly. If this is difficult then set up an autoresponder to confirm you have received their enquiry/payment and will get back to them within a few hours.

Place references that you have received from past customers to show that you are a professional company.

Your challenge will be to be listed in the major search engines and then get traffic. Now market your web site like mad. It will take several months to make an impact in the major search engines. So build up your local custom whilst you are doing this. www.GetIntoGoogleFast.com – Does exactly what is says in the domain!

An Internet Marketing Strategy

Ok, you've got your web site set up, you are sure that it is search engine friendly and you are pretty certain what your customers want. You've identified at least 3 services that you want to promote and you think that they meet your potential customer's needs. So now what?

Well unfortunately the days, that I can remember, of "build it and they will come" have long gone. Unless you promote your web site – no one will know that you are there and no visitors means no sales. So where so you go from here?

Well take a deep breath, a pen and paper and let's start on your Marketing Strategy. Briefly for a new business, with a relatively inexperienced marketer, your strategy will probably include the following options:
- Pay Per Click Advertising
- Article Marketing
- Email Marketing
- Community Marketing
- Classified Advertising

So let's get started – and before you start panicking, you are just writing your Marketing Strategy. This chapter will explain how to do all of the following.

Internet Advertising Kit

For each of your programs/services

- Write a short advert – say 50 words.
- Write a very short advert – say 15 words
- Write a short article – say about 400 – 600 words.
- Decide on your keywords – say about 30 – 50 words.

Internet Marketing Kit

For your web site theme

- Write at least 6 short auto responder messages.
- Find or write at least 2 giveaway services.

Internet Marketing Tools

- Your web site
- An autoresponder
- A good email account

Internet Marketing Strategy

Now let's put all of these together into your first Marketing Strategy.

1. **Submit your web site to all the major search engines.** This will start to get your web site noticed. As this takes a long time, it needs to be the first thing that you do. You can do this yourself or pay someone else to do this for you. We provide this service for our customers for £20 a month, which includes submission to Google, Yahoo and MSN.

2. **Set up your autoresponder form** on your web site and load your messages into the autoresponder. Ensure that you offer one of the giveaway services as a bonus for signing onto your ezine. The second giveaway can be set up for message 3 or 4. Your messages should be sent in the following intervals. Day 1,3,7,7,7,7

   3. **Set up your download pages**, for your bonus services as well as the services you are selling. Ensure that you provide an extra offer on each download page.

4. **Submit your article** – including your resource box, to about 6 major ezine article sites. Limit yourself to 6 at the moment. Each of these submissions, if accepted will give you a link to your web site. If too many links to your new web site appear very quickly, search engines assume that you have been using "black hat" SEO tactics (a total no no) and will not list your site.

5. **Identify 4 forums** that discuss the topics of your web site. Set yourself up an account name that describes you well. We use the name "Biz Guru" which is our trade mark and name. Set up your signature to include your web site address. You now have 4 good links to your web site.

6. **Answer Questions:** Start answering questions asked within the forums. Do NOT post adverts for your web site or services. Use this time to establish your credentials. If you answer questions well and contribute to the forums, your web site tag will be noticed.

7. **Set up a PPC campaign** – you can start with the smaller search engines first. Take your very small advert and your keywords and use them in your campaign. Most search engines will help you with your choice of keywords. Remember to set a budget and test, test and test again until you get quality and converting traffic.

8. **Set up some classified ads**. You can do this one of two ways: i) choose one or two major sites/email lists and advertise with them. ii) use an ezine ad blaster to send your ad out to numerous lower quality places.

9. **Test, Update and Modify**. Review, change and add to your PPC keywords. Submit more articles and adverts. Start tactfully promoting your services in the forums.

Well that's what to do to be a success. Good Luck.

Secrets of Success

Probably one of the greatest secrets of success with this kind of sales operation is that in order to make the sales, and talk about large sales at parties, you must have the widest selection of merchandise possible.

Many beginners, not understanding that offering the potential buyers a wide and varied selection of items to choose from is what builds your profits in a hurry, base their entire merchandising plan around a selection that's of special interest or particularly appealing to themselves. It's all right to include the items that you especially like, but don't base your entire merchandise line on the things you like; you're selling to others, not yourself!

Most successful Party Selling merchandisers advise that you should display at least forty different items and more if you have the supplier contacts or the buying expertise. The actual decisions on which products to carry and display at your parties should be based upon these four factors:

1) The kinds of gift items, personal decor articles, and general merchandise the people in your area are buying.
2) The styles or fads currently in vogue in your area.
3) Contacts with enough suppliers who can furnish you with the kind of merchandise your potential buyers want.

4) Your ability to shop among the various suppliers, and verify that you are getting the very best merchandise value obtainable.

Still another important point to consider before buying merchandise to display and sell: Do the prices you are paying for your products wholesale, allow you enough room for a reasonable profit when compared to your time and expense?

Do some market research relative to your ambitions; get answers to the questions we've set forth for you, and when you're satisfied that you understand the workings of Party Selling merchandising, grab the opportunity and run with it!

Brought to You By The Biz Guru

"If you need help with your business – click or brick – we're here to help"

www.StartMyNewBusiness.com

Index:

www.ingramcontent.com/pod-product-compliance
Lightning Source LLC
Chambersburg PA
CBHW021916190326
41519CB00008B/796